BE A MAGICIAN OF YOUR LIFE

"Be ready to join the journey into the world of magic, where you can transform your life and become a Magician of your own life. Conquer Challenges, Master Time, Ignite Self-Belief, & from Imagination to Gratitude, embrace the magic within you."

RAHUL PARMAR

TABLE OF CONTENTS

   - Understanding the Impact of Attitude

   - Cultivating Self-Belief

   - Time as a Precious Resource

   - Effective Time Management Strategies

   - Overcoming Procrastination

   - The Art of Taking Initiative

Preface

Welcome to "Be a Magician of Your Life," a transformative journey designed to unlock the secrets of personal empowerment and magical living. As the author of this enchanting guide, I am thrilled to embark on this exploration of self-discovery, positivity, and the manifestation of dreams.

In this book, we will delve into the realms of positive attitude, self-belief, and the invaluable essence of time. You'll be encouraged to embrace action, steering clear of procrastination, and witness the magic that unfolds when you become an active participant in your own destiny.

Prepare to unlock the doors to the extraordinary with "The Secret Power of Imagination & Affirmation," where the art and science of manifesting your dreams will be unraveled. We will navigate the fascinating territory of the Law of Attraction in "Discovering the Magic," and explore the profound impact of "Self-Realization."

As you journey through these pages, you'll find a roadmap to personal transformation in the concluding chapter, "Embracing the Magic of

Transformation." This is more than just a book; it's a guide to a life enriched with love, gratitude, and self-motivation.

"The Enchantment of Life's Essence" will invite you to explore the depths of love, affection, and gratitude, while "Be Your Own Mentor" ignites the flame of self-motivation within you. Lastly, in "Beyond Words," I express my heartfelt gratitude to you, my enchanting readers, for joining me on this magical odyssey.

Each chapter is meticulously crafted to empower you, providing not just insights but actionable steps to become the magician of your own life. So, open your heart, engage your mind, and let the enchantment begin.

Wishing you a magical journey ahead!

Rahul Parmar

Bangalore, India

Introduction: Be a Magician of Your Life

Welcome to the realm of limitless possibilities, where you possess the power to shape your destiny and weave the fabric of your dream life. Thank you, everyone, for investing your valuable time in reading this book. In the grand scheme of things, time is the most precious entity in the world.

🕐 **Value of Time: **

Often, we relentlessly chase after money, believing it to be the essence of life. However, beyond monetary value, our time is the most priceless possession. Everything bestowed upon us by nature is invaluable, yet we often fail to recognize the significance of free things.

**Regrets and Realization: **

Sometimes, we only grasp the importance of those free gifts from the divine after squandering them. Whether it's good health, a pleasant environment, a sharp mind, or just time itself, once gone, they cannot be repurchased, no matter how much money we possess.

**Wake-Up Call: **

This book aims to serve as a wake-up call, urging each reader to understand the profound significance of every second. Those reading this book are making use of each crucial moment.

**Reader Connection: **

I feel a genuine connection with each of you, as this is not just a one-way reading experience. I'm communicating with you directly, one-to-one.

**Personal Commitment: **

My purpose is for you to make a commitment to yourself to utilize every second of your life effectively. The words written here are not just for reading; they are a pact with yourself to enhance your life.

😟 **Self-Reflection: **

As I express these thoughts, I'm contemplating and jotting down ideas here. I invite you to promise that whatever insights I share ahead, you'll follow and implement in your life. My goal is for this book to bring about some positive changes in your life. If it manages to impact even 10 percent of your life, it would be my greatest achievement.

👣 **Journey of Change: **

The purpose of this book is to guide you through essential aspects of life. Your commitment to read this book is an investment in transforming your life. I've highlighted crucial elements that genuinely matter for anyone looking to change their life.

🌟 **Reader's Pledge: **

I expect a commitment from you. After reading this book, either you bring about a positive change in your life, or I consider it a significant failure. Every word in this book is meticulously chosen, focusing on the practical aspects of life transformation.

📖 **Reading Approach: **

Approach this book differently. Unlike conventional reading, avoid reading during routine tasks. Dedicate focused time, ensuring full immersion. Visualize the concepts, feel my presence as I communicate these thoughts directly to you.

🎲 **Seriousness of Life: **

This book is in your hands because you take your life seriously. Today, as you read, millions of youth might be scrolling through social media, but you are investing your time in something significant.

🦉 **Self-Inquiry: **

When delving into these ideas, ask yourself if you can connect with them. To absorb this book effectively, read it in solitude, following each piece of advice. Before diving in, challenge yourself with a fundamental question: Do you believe that nothing in the world is impossible, and if someone else can do it, so can you? Recognize that everyone is bestowed with the same potential; it's how we utilize that power that matters.

🌐 **Unified Power: **

Consider this: God has endowed everyone with the same energy. How you wield that power depends on you. Acknowledge this truth to yourself. Start this journey with a formation of purpose, united with unwavering belief. I promise you'll embark on a transformative path. In life, many things are known to us intellectually, but feeling and realizing them are distinct. For instance, you may know about an upcoming exam, but realizing its importance as a milestone in your life can be a game-changer.

**Significance of Realization: **

This is where my role comes in. I aim to make you feel every aspect crucial for life transformation. Connect with the material as if I'm communicating directly with you. Your dreams and visions should be visualized, felt, and realized. This book is in your hands because you take life seriously, unlike countless individuals spending time on social media.

**Initiate the Journey: **

So, let's start this journey with the hope that this book will instigate substantial changes in your life. You won't read it casually; instead, treat it like a sacred text. Absorb each word, visualizing its impact on your life. The commitment to connect with me, visualize the content, and follow through is paramount. Every point emphasized in this book is essential for your success parameters.

**Personal Transformation: **

Create a physical representation of your dreams and formations. Pen down your aspirations on paper, place them on a notice board, and integrate them into your life. Make the connection between your actions and the reason behind them. Reasons hold immense importance in life. They drive individuals from humble backgrounds to achieve extraordinary milestones.

**Direction Matters: **

Hard work is undeniably crucial, but direction is equally vital. Align your efforts in the right direction, and you might achieve more with less effort. This book's purpose is to guide you in finding that direction. As you read each page, question yourself: What have I learned? When will I start implementing this in my life?

🎯 **Commit to Change: **

Remember, the journey's commencement lies in your hands. You are dedicating time to read this book, a clear indication of your seriousness about life. The book serves as a guide, directing you toward clarity of purpose and effective actions. It's an opportunity to transform your life, one that you're not taking lightly. Take the first step towards making your dreams a reality. Once you decide to commit to change, you're on the verge of becoming the magician of your dream life.

**Closing Message: **

So, make a promise to yourself to create a better life. As you embark on this journey through the book, remember that every second counts. The communication here is not just through words but a direct exchange between us.

"Introduction About the Author"*

"Introduction to the Journey"

"Embarking on a Journey: Unveiling the Author's Odyssey"

Greetings, dear readers, as we embark on a profound journey together. Within these pages, I invite you to explore the tapestry of my life—a narrative woven through trials, triumphs, and the transformative power of resilience. This book is more than just words on paper; it is the unveiling of my personal odyssey—a journey that took me from the challenges of an average student to the fulfilling role of an author.

Section 1: "Hello, Let's Begin"

Dear reader, let us dive into the depths of my story—a story that echoes with the struggles of my childhood, particularly when my father retired from the army during my 10th-grade exams. Despite financial challenges and average academic performance, I persevered in education while shouldering work responsibilities. This journey led me through the realms of computer hardware, networking, and eventually, a significant chapter at Mahendra Coaching Private Limited, where I later became a successful trainer and faculty of reasoning for bank & SSC competitive exams.

Section 2: "Exploring Teaching and Inspiring Change"

My experiences at Mahendra Coaching Private Limited and the subsequent transition unfolded not just as a professional journey but as a profound exploration of teaching. This section delves into the impact of these experiences on students, the education system, and life itself. Beyond showcasing highlights, this book aspires to inspire positive change by illuminating the struggles and lessons learned along the way.

Dear reader, I extend an invitation to dive into the deeper layers of my journey. Uncover motivations, confront challenges, and witness the metamorphosis that has sculpted my life. Consider this book a promise to make your investment of time immensely worthwhile. Share it with friends, and I sincerely thank you for the profound significance you grant to this endeavor.

Section 3: "A Glimpse into the Early Years"

Embark on a journey through the formative years of my life, born into challenges, navigating schooling under the guidance of the CBSE board. Despite facing financial constraints, my academic performance, though average, did not deter me from pursuing education while simultaneously shouldering work responsibilities. Navigating the professional terrain, I not only completed my graduation but also delved into the intricacies of computer hardware and networking.

Section 4: "From Teaching at Mahendra Coaching to a Fresh Beginning"

The narrative unfolds further, shedding light on my teaching sojourn at Mahendra Coaching Private Limited. It reflects on the profound impact these experiences had on students, the education landscape, and the essence of life itself. Joining the State Bank of India marked not an end but a fresh beginning. Engaging in the home loan business, I made significant contributions to my branch & A.O.

Section 5: "Weaving the Tapestry of Teaching"

Embark with me on the next chapter of my journey, where I guide you through my role as a reasoning faculty at Mahendra Coaching Private Limited—a pivotal period in my professional odyssey. This section intricately delves into the art of imparting knowledge, reflecting on the transformation from the classroom to contributing significantly to the success of my branch at the State Bank of India.

Section 6: "The Essence of Transformation"

In this chapter, we delve deep into the essence of transformation, unveiling how these experiences have not only shaped my professional identity but also left an indelible mark on the lives of those I've had the privilege to encounter. It's not merely a recounting of events but an exploration of the profound impact that teaching and the banking landscape can have on individuals and the broader spectrum of life.

Section 7: "Inviting You to a Transformative Journey"

Consider this book as a heartfelt invitation to plunge into the depths of my life. Beyond the surface narrative, it beckons you to navigate the intricate details of my journey, revealing the raw authenticity of struggles and the profound lessons extracted along the way. The aspiration is not just to share success stories but also to expose the vulnerabilities that underpin the path to triumph, fostering a shared understanding of the transformative power within us all.

Embark with me on this transformative odyssey. Uncover the layers that define my narrative, explore the intricacies that molded my character, and join me in reflecting on the profound tapestry of life. Your investment of time in these pages is a commitment I deeply value, and I extend my sincere gratitude for choosing to be an integral part of this expedition.

<u>Section 8: "Culmination of a Lifelong Odyssey"</u>

This chapter unfolds the next phase of my journey at the State Bank of India, where I immersed myself in the realm of home loans, contributing significantly to the success of my Branch/AO and Circle. As we conclude this odyssey through the pages of my life, I extend a sincere promise to make your investment in this book worthwhile.

Section 9: "A Promise to Readers"

The stories shared, lessons learned, and insights gained are not just mine but ours to ponder upon. This section encapsulates a commitment to authenticity, aiming to resonate with each reader on a personal level.

Section 10: "Gratitude and Conclusion"

In the final chapter, gratitude takes center stage. I express heartfelt thanks for your invaluable time and attention. Your decision to embark on this literary voyage alongside me is a gesture I cherish deeply. As we bid adieu to these pages, my hope is that the essence of my journey lingers in your thoughts, sparking inspiration and perhaps even igniting transformative ripples in your own story.

Your support and engagement in this endeavor are the cornerstones of its significance. From the bottom of my heart, thank you. "

Acknowledgment

"Hello friends,

I would like to express my heartfelt gratitude to several individuals who played a special role in the success of this book and motivated me throughout the journey of successful book writing. I stand before you today with a profound sense of gratitude and humility as I express my thanks to the individuals who have been instrumental in shaping the journey of this book. The path to becoming an author is often solitary, but the support and encouragement I've received have been anything but. I extend my heartfelt appreciation to those who have played a pivotal role in this literary endeavor.

**1. Family - The Pillars of Strength: **

First and foremost, I want to extend my sincere thanks to my family members, especially my parents and my younger brother, along with all relatives and loved ones. Their encouragement and support have been crucial in shaping my decision to embark on this authorial journey. In the grand tapestry of life, family forms the foundational threads. I also extend my deepest gratitude to my parents, whose unwavering support and blessings have been the bedrock of my accomplishments. To my brother, whose encouragement has been a constant motivator, and to all my extended family members, I offer sincere thanks for being the pillars of my strength.

**2. Dedicated to My Precious Ones: **

This book is dedicated to my Late Grandfather and Late Grandmother, along with my Maternal Grandparents, my Parents, my Younger Brother, My Better Half – Aarushi Singh, my best friend as well as my elder brother who one of the biggest well-wishers of mine - Santosh Sir. My heartfelt gratitude extends to my two precious gems and assets of my life - my both sons, Yuvraj Singh, who is presently 6 years old, and my cutie pie lucky charm, Dhruv Singh, who is 6 months old.

**3. Gratitude to Everyone: **

I express gratitude to all my colleagues, seniors, teachers, relatives, neighbors, all home loan customers, all my friends (Specially one of my close friend Late Ramveer Sir, Delhi Police, S.I) and Siddharth Panchal (Senior Pilot, Indigo Airlines) & finally, all my lovable students. Your support and encouragement have been the driving force behind the completion of this book. Each one of you holds a special place in my heart, and I am truly thankful for your unwavering support.

**4. The Spousal Support - A Source of Inspiration: **

Behind every successful endeavor is a supportive partner, and in my case, it is my beloved wife, my Angel (as I called her lovingly). Deepest thanks to my wife (Aarushi Singh), a beacon of grace and strength, whose unwavering belief in my aspirations has been my guiding star. She not only serves as a companion but also as a muse, infusing the narrative of my pursuits with inspiration and resilience. Her presence is not just a companionate bond but a source of inspiration that fuels the narrative of my pursuits. In her, I find both muse and confidante.

Her unwavering belief in my abilities and encouragement have been the driving force behind my pursuit of this literary venture. To her, I owe a debt of gratitude beyond words. She is one of the Guardian Angels of my life. Without any doubt, I can say that she is the best gift of my life from God's side as a life partner & mentor.

**5. Friendship and Mentorship: **

A special mention is reserved for my dear friend, Santosh MB, who has been not just a companion but a mentor. His insights and shared experiences have added invaluable depth to my understanding of life.

Mentorship is a gift, and I've been fortunate to have inspirational figures like him in my life. To Santosh, a friend whose wisdom and camaraderie have been a constant, I extend my thanks. In the realm of mentorship, his role surpasses the conventional, enriching my narrative with shared experiences and profound insights. In acknowledging friends, I recognize the threads that weave the fabric of my personal growth. He is the Another Guardian Angel of my life along with my wife, no doubt that as a friend, brother & mentor he is one of the best GEM ever I have from my GOD.

**6. Professional Encouragement - From Mentors to Colleagues: **

The professional chapters of my life are illuminated by mentors who not only imparted knowledge but also sculpted my professional ethos. First & Foremost I express my sincere gratitude to all the seniors and mentors in my professional life, especially to honorable Mr. Murali Krishna Sir, General Manager of State Bank of India, Chennai Circle, who provided me with great inspiration during my tenure in Bangalore when he was DGM (B&O) in Bangalore.

A word from a mentor or boss can change your life, and his words always motivated me. So, through this book, I want to extend my thanks to Mr. Murali Krishna sir for his profound impact on my life during his tenure as the DGM, AO3 in Bangalore. His motivational words always resonated with me and played a pivotal role in my journey. Moreover, at the initial levels of my career, a beacon of leadership during my tenure in Bangalore, as well as to honorable CGM Farooq Sir.

"I always recall these powerful lines when a high-ranking senior official of India's largest bank says, 'Rahul, even I find motivation from you in front of everyone and during meetings. It means a lot to me, and I gain so much motivation and confidence. From here, I draw inspiration to do something that will motivate everyone and set the right direction. I feel highly blessed to have senior officials and mentors like him.' A word from a mentor or boss can change your life, and his words have consistently motivated me". So, through this book, I want to extend my thanks to Mr. Murali Krishna sir for his profound impact on my life during his tenure as the DGM, AO3 in Bangalore. His motivational words always resonated with me and played a pivotal role in my journey. Moreover, at the initial levels of my career, a beacon of leadership during my tenure in Bangalore, as well as to honorable CGM Farooq Sir."

Present DGM (B&O) Bangalore, AO2, Pradeep Nair sir who immensely & unconditionally support me after Murali Krishna sir and stood as another idol in SBI after Murali Krishna sir, Special Thanks to Regional Manager of RBO3 Surendra T K Sir who always stands with me as a strong pillar of my life whenever I find difficulties & faces challenges in my professional life whose leadership has been a guiding light for me & Chief Manager Rajith Shetty sir who has been instrumental in creating a conducive environment for growth. I appreciate the collective efforts of everyone in my professional circle who has contributed to my personal and professional development.

"I also want to extend special thanks to Honorable GM Sir & CGM Sir of Bangalore Circle, as well as all my HLST team members of Bangalore North & South, including all my HLST AGM's. Special mention goes to my 1st AGM when I joined HLST in 2019, Sanjeev Kulkarni Sir, for his incredible support. I'd also like to express my gratitude to other AGMs like AGM Jay Gopal Sir, Lokesh Sir, and Kush Sir, including present AGM's of HLST. I appreciate the support from other professional colleagues like Ankit Sir (SBI, Sainagar BM), Varun Sir (SBI, Sahakar Nagar BM), Kamlesh Yadav Sir (SBI RACPC Yelahanka), and RBO 2 RM Madam, i.e., Manikyamba Madam, who fostered an environment conducive to growth."

**7. Readers and Students - The Ultimate Motivators: **

A book finds its purpose in the hands of readers, and to all those who have taken the time to engage with my work, I express my profound gratitude. A book's essence lies in the hands of its readers. To those who have engaged with my work, I extend profound appreciation. To my students, whose relentless curiosity and vigor have been a wellspring of motivation, I express heartfelt thanks. In their interaction, I find the pulse of purpose in my endeavors. To my students, whose enthusiasm and curiosity have been a constant motivator, I extend a special thank you. Your presence in my life has been transformative.

The journey of this book has been a profound odyssey enriched by the intricate threads of relationships, experiences, and shared wisdom. To everyone who has left an indelible mark, whether through personal bonds or professional collaborations, I extend a depth of gratitude that transcends the limitations of words.

I extend my thanks to all the students I have had the privilege to teach. Your motivation has contributed significantly to my life, and I consider you all my real teachers. My readers, followers, students, boss, mentors, family members, and my best friend, Mr. Santosh MB & my beautiful soulmate, My Angel deserve heartfelt thanks.

In conclusion, the journey of writing this book has been enriched by the tapestry of relationships, experiences, and shared wisdom. To everyone who has been a part of this voyage, whether in a personal or professional capacity, I extend my deepest appreciation.

8. Copyright Disclaimer and Thanks Message to Amazon:

I extend my gratitude to Amazon for their support in the publication and distribution of this book, and a special thanks for providing the ISBN. This book is protected by copyright law, and any unauthorized reproduction, distribution, or use of the material without written permission from the author is strictly prohibited.

In conclusion, the journey of writing this book has been enriched by the tapestry of relationships, experiences, and shared wisdom. To everyone who has been a part of this voyage, whether in a personal or professional capacity, I extend my deepest appreciation.

I extend my heartfelt thanks to all my loving students whom I have had the privilege to teach, as well as all my customers and all my readers. Your motivation has contributed significantly to my life, and I consider you all my real teachers. In particular, my readers, followers, students, boss, mentors, family members, and my best friend, Mr. Santosh, deserve heartfelt thanks.

Once Again Big thank you to everyone who holds a status in my life and to all my readers. If you gain something valuable from this book, it would be a tremendous gift in return for your unwavering support. Once again, thank you very much.

Thank you!

Rahul Parmar

Power of Positive Attitude & Self Belief

Setting the Stage for Takeoff - "Strap in for Flight"

Ready for Flight: Secure the seatbelt tight around your waist, for the journey you're about to embark on will take you to the path your heart has longed for years. This isn't just a physical journey; it's a profound expedition into the uncharted territories of your mind and soul. As you fasten your seatbelt, visualize it as a symbolic act of securing your commitment to self-discovery and transformation.

Dreams Unleashed: You are on the verge of fulfilling your dreams, navigating the right course. Imagine your dreams as majestic birds waiting to soar into the limitless sky. This journey is about unleashing those dreams, letting them take flight, and guiding them to destinations you once thought were beyond reach. The runway is clear, and the control tower of your mind is ready for takeoff.

Initiating with Confidence - "Magic, Solutions, and Positive Perspectives"

Dual Commencement: Introducing two essential elements - confidence and a positive outlook - because anything I share involves magic, solutions, and begins with your belief. Confidence is the fuel that propels you forward, and a positive outlook is the compass guiding your path. Together, they form the alchemy of success. The magic lies in the synergy between your unwavering belief and the actionable solutions you'll encounter on this transformative journey.

Book in Your Hands: The book is in your hands because you want to change your life, investing time into it. But, do you have a hundred percent belief in yourself to accomplish any task or fulfill your dreams? Consider this book as your personal flight manual, and each word as a navigational beacon. Trust in the process, and the takeoff will be nothing short of extraordinary.

Questioning Beliefs - "Self-Interrogation and Visionary Confidence"

Self-Questioning Journey: Challenge yourself with a question: Can you seriously achieve anything you dream of? Close your eyes, concentrate on your chosen deity, and ask if you have the confidence to fulfill your vision. This self-interrogation isn't about doubt but about acknowledging and reinforcing your capabilities. The journey of self-discovery begins with fearless questions that lead to visionary confidence.

Crossing the First Stage: If the answer is yes, you've crossed the first stage. Now, you can proceed with the journey. If it's no, it's time to upgrade yourself. Understand that the first stage isn't a barrier but a checkpoint. It's where you acknowledge your starting point and envision the limitless possibilities that lie ahead.

Self-Confidence and Positive Outlook - "Upgrading Yourself"

The Power Within: Believe in yourself first, as the things you envision go beyond realism. Your limitations define your thoughts. The first step is self-confidence, followed by a positive perspective. Imagine self-confidence as the ignition switch that activates the powerhouse within you, and positive outlook as the compass that guides your flight through challenges.

Two Types of Readers: There are two kinds of readers - those who believe in themselves, maintaining a positive attitude. They think, "I can change my life. It's in my hands to shape my family's life. I can bid farewell to poverty or create a legacy while being wealthy." It's all about attitude. Your attitude determines not only the altitude of your dreams but also the depth of your impact on the world.

Unlocking Potential - "Tapping into the Reservoir of Infinite Possibilities"

Visualization Techniques: Picture your goals vividly. See them not just as distant aspirations but as tangible realities. Visualization is the bridge between your present and your desired future. Envision success, feel the emotions associated with achievement, and let this mental rehearsal propel you forward.

Affirmation Mastery: Harness the power of positive affirmations. Craft statements that resonate with your goals and aspirations. Repeat them with conviction, and watch how your subconscious mind internalizes these affirmations, aligning your thoughts, actions, and beliefs with the reality you wish to create.

Adapting to Challenges: Understand that challenges are not roadblocks but steppingstones on your journey. Cultivate resilience and adaptability. A positive attitude doesn't deny the existence of challenges; it thrives despite them. Embrace setbacks as lessons, pivot when necessary, and let challenges fuel your determination.

Conclusion: "Success in Positivity"

Final Thoughts: Your successful life depends on your self-belief and a positive perspective. Manifesting your dream life starts with crossing the first stage, and then upgrading yourself through self-confidence and a positive outlook. This journey is not a sprint but a marathon, and every step forward is a triumph. Embrace the magic of your positive attitude and self-belief, for they are the wings that will carry you to heights you've only dared to imagine.

Unlocking Potential: As you delve into the essence of positive attitude and self-belief, remember that you are not merely reading a book; you are unlocking the potential within yourself. Visualization, affirmation mastery, and adaptability are the keys to tap into the reservoir of infinite possibilities. Picture your success, affirm your capabilities, and navigate through challenges with resilience.

Your journey is a dynamic process, and as you soar higher, keep in mind that every chapter you read is a steppingstone toward your personal transformation. This book is a guide, but the true magic happens when you internalize these principles and apply them to your life. The power of positive attitude and self-belief isn't just theoretical; it's a force that shapes your reality. May this journey lead you to success in positivity, and may you discover the boundless potential that resides within you. 🚀

Know the Value of your Time

"The Profound Impact of Time: Harnessing its Power for Transformation"

Greetings, my dear readers! In the preceding chapters, we explored the critical concepts of self-belief, maintaining a positive attitude, and understanding their transformative potential. Now, let's embark on a profound journey into the quintessence of life – the value of time.

**Introduction to the Intrinsic Worth of Time: **

In our modern, fast-paced lives, time often seems to slip through our fingers, unnoticed and underappreciated. However, comprehending the intrinsic value of time is pivotal for anyone seeking a holistic transformation in their life. Unlike material possessions, time is a finite resource, and once spent, it can never be reclaimed.

**Time as a Catalyst for Complete Transformation: **

To achieve a comprehensive metamorphosis in our lives, acknowledging the catalytic role of time is imperative. Each passing moment presents an opportunity for growth, learning, and progress. When harnessed effectively, time becomes the driving force behind personal and professional development.

**The Dual Nature of Free Offerings: **

Free offerings, be it good health, relationships, or time, often bear a dual nature. Their accessibility may lead us to overlook their significance. However, just like time, these intangible assets are priceless. Recognizing this duality allows us to elevate our perspective and accord them the priority they deserve.

**Time – Beyond a Linear Concept: **

Time is not merely a linear concept measured in hours, minutes, and seconds. It is a dynamic force, capable of shaping our destinies. Understanding time as a multidimensional entity enables us to navigate its intricacies and make deliberate choices that align with our goals.

**The Financial Analogy: **

Drawing parallels between our attitude towards time and finances can be enlightening. While we meticulously manage our financial resources, often neglecting free offerings, extending the same diligence to our time investment can be transformative. A loss of an hour, much like a financial setback, reverberates throughout our day.

**The Essence of Self-Empowerment: **

Cultivating an attitude that recognizes time as a precious commodity empowers us to take control of our lives. By embracing the uniqueness of our time and investing it judiciously, we set the stage for personal growth and fulfillment.

**The Transience of Enthusiasm: **

Enthusiasm, that fleeting burst of motivation, is transient. It's essential to differentiate between momentary josh and sustained dedication. While external motivation has its place, internalizing the commitment to utilize our time wisely is paramount for lasting success.

**Success and the Rarity of Easy Paths: **

Success is not a facile journey; it demands dedication, perseverance, and a distinctive approach to life. If success were easily attainable, it would cease to be an accomplishment. Successful individuals stand out precisely because they have chosen to live their lives differently.

**A Call to Action: **

As we navigate the complexities of life, let us internalize the profound impact of time. Let us view each moment as an investment, recognizing that its value extends beyond the immediate. By embracing this perspective, we position ourselves to seize opportunities, learn from experiences, and navigate the twists and turns of our unique journeys.

"Time's Symphony: A Melody of Moments that Mold Destiny"

Greetings, dear readers! In our quest for a richer life, we've explored self-belief, positivity, and the transformative potential of attitude. Now, let's unravel the intricate symphony of time, where each note plays a pivotal role in shaping the destiny of our existence.

**The Pendulum of Opportunity: **

Imagine time as a grand pendulum swinging ceaselessly, presenting us with unique opportunities at each oscillation. The challenge lies not in the swing itself but in recognizing and capitalizing on the opportunities it unveils. The story of success often intertwines with those who seized the moment when the pendulum swung their way.

Example: Consider the tale of J.K. Rowling, who, amidst personal struggles and rejections, seized the opportune moment to birth the magical world of Harry Potter. Her journey reflects the power of leveraging time's oscillations to transform adversity into triumph.

Time as a Canvas:

Envision time as an expansive canvas, awaiting the brushstrokes of our actions and decisions. Each stroke contributes to the masterpiece that is our life. Neglecting the canvas may result in an incomplete or uninspiring picture, while deliberate and thoughtful strokes lead to a tapestry of fulfillment.

Example: Think of Elon Musk, whose strategic decisions across ventures like Tesla and SpaceX were not impulsive but carefully painted on the canvas of time. His journey exemplifies how meticulous strokes, well-timed, can shape industries and redefine possibilities.

The Compounding Effect of Time:

Much like compound interest in finance, the value of our actions compounds over time. Small, consistent efforts yield exponential results. This compounding effect is a force that, when harnessed, propels us towards unprecedented achievements.

Example: Warren Buffett, the legendary investor, is a living testament to the compounding effect of time. His patient and consistent investment strategies over decades have transformed him into one of the wealthiest individuals globally.

Time's Role in Innovation:

Innovation, the driving force of progress, thrives on the sands of time. It is the intersection of ideas, persistence, and the right moment. Those who revolutionize industries understand the significance of timing, syncing their innovations with societal needs.

Example: The advent of the iPhone by Apple under Steve Jobs wasn't merely about technology; it was about timing. The smartphone revolutionized communication, and its success was deeply intertwined with being the right product at the right time.

Time's Healing Touch:

Life brings challenges and setbacks, but time acts as a soothing balm. It possesses the extraordinary ability to heal wounds, mend broken spirits, and offer the clarity required for resilient comebacks.

Example: Oprah Winfrey's journey from a traumatic childhood to becoming a media mogul illustrates the healing power of time. Her transformative evolution showcases how time, coupled with resilience, can turn pain into strength.

Time's Dichotomy: Friend or Foe:

Time, a paradoxical entity, can be both a friend and a foe. Embracing its friendship involves using it judiciously, recognizing its opportunities. Treating it as a foe entails procrastination and missed chances. The choice is ours.

Example: Consider the contrasting tales of two entrepreneurs. One, by seizing timely opportunities, builds an empire. The other, plagued by procrastination, watches as opportunities slip away.

The Ripple Effect of Choices:

Consider each choice as a pebble cast into the pond of time. The ripples extend far beyond our immediate vision, touching the shores of our destiny. Acknowledging the profound ripple effect empowers us to make choices that resonate positively through the corridors of time.

Example: Rosa Parks, with a single act of defiance on a Montgomery bus, created ripples that reverberated through the Civil Rights Movement.

Her choice echoed through time, shaping the course of history.

Time's Silent Witness to Evolution:

Time silently bears witness to the evolution of individuals and societies. It is an observer of our triumphs, struggles, and the collective journey of humanity. Recognizing time as a silent witness encourages us to contribute positively to its ongoing narrative.

Example: The transformation of Nelson Mandela from prisoner to president is a testament to the profound impact of time. His journey mirrors the evolution of a nation and its people over decades.

The Tapestry of Relationships:

Our relationships are threads woven into the fabric of time. Nurturing these threads with care and consideration contributes to a tapestry of meaningful connections. Understanding that relationships are not isolated moments but continuous threads in time fosters enduring bonds.

Example: The enduring friendship between C.S. Lewis and J.R.R. Tolkien, two literary giants, shaped not only their individual lives but also the literary landscape of their time. Their connection echoes through the pages of history.

Time's Classroom of Learning:

Every moment in time offers lessons waiting to be learned. Embracing life's continuous learning process allows us to evolve, adapt, and thrive. Each experience, whether triumphant or challenging, contributes to our growth.

Example: Marie Curie's tireless pursuit of knowledge and her groundbreaking discoveries in the field of science exemplify the idea of time as a relentless classroom. Her dedication to learning echoes through generations of scientists.

The Legacy We Inscribe in Time:

Consider time as a vast parchment on which we inscribe our legacy. Our actions, values, and contributions become the ink that leaves an indelible mark. Consciously crafting a positive legacy ensures that our influence persists beyond our physical presence.

Example: Mahatma Gandhi's legacy as a proponent of nonviolent resistance continues to inspire movements for justice and freedom. His principles, inscribed in the annals of time, echo in the pursuit of civil rights worldwide.

Time's Dance with Creativity:

Creativity dances hand in hand with time. Artists, innovators, and visionaries channel the essence of their era into timeless creations. Understanding this symbiotic relationship allows us to appreciate the cultural echoes that reverberate through the ages.

Example: William Shakespeare, through his timeless plays, captured the essence of the Elizabethan era. His creativity transcends time, resonating with audiences across centuries.

**Conclusion - Embracing Time's Eternal Embrace: **

In conclusion, dear readers, let us embrace time not as a fleeting acquaintance but as an eternal embrace. Its unseen influence, like echoes in the vast canyon of eternity, shapes our individual and collective destinies.

Thank you for joining me on this exploration of time's profound impact, from the symphony of moments to the echoes that transcend the boundaries of the present. May your journey through time be adorned with wisdom, purpose, and the beauty of everlasting echoes!

Be An Action-Taker and Avoid Procrastination

"Transforming Thoughts into Deeds: The Power of Action-Taking"

Greetings, dear readers! As we delve deeper into the concept of becoming an "Action-Taker and Avoider," we uncover the intricate process of translating thoughts into tangible actions. In the vast landscape of ideas and aspirations, the bridge between ideation and execution often remains elusive. The essence of becoming an "Action-Taker" takes center stage, propelling us from contemplation to concrete realization.

Consider the common goal of waking up early, a shared aspiration for many. The mental image of rising at dawn is crystal clear, and the benefits are vividly understood. However, the challenge lies not in the clarity of this mental image but in the ability to translate it into daily reality. Here, the "Action-Taker" seizes control, setting the alarm for 5 AM and ensuring that each morning begins at the desired time. In contrast, the "Avoider" may linger in the comforting warmth of the bed, perpetually delaying the moment of action.

Let's exemplify this through the narrative of Abhinay, who resolved to change his habit of waking up late. Enthusiastically inspired by motivational videos, the initial decision faced roadblocks in practical implementation. The surge of motivation acted as a fleeting burst of energy, but the true challenge emerged the next morning. Despite the intention to wake up at 5 AM, the habitual snoozing of the alarm persisted. This highlights the gap between envisioning positive change and taking concrete steps towards it.

Now, extend this scenario to the individual contemplating a career change or entrepreneurship. The thought process is intense, and a clear vision is painted in the mind. However, the transition from ideation to execution demands a shift from being an "Avoider" to an "Action-Taker." Until the first step is taken, mental deliberations remain trapped in the realm of wishful thinking.

Let's explore the analogy of Prakash, symbolizing challenges or awards. Prakash often tends to be avoided due to the inherent discomfort associated with stepping out of one's comfort zone. An individual aspiring to shed weight might consistently evade the challenge of regular exercise, succumbing to the allure of the familiar routine. However, it's the action-taker who embraces the discomfort, hits the gym, and triumphs over Prakash.

Consider the professional realm where a daunting project looms large. The avoider might procrastinate, delay decisions, and evade the challenge. On the contrary, the action-taker acknowledges the pressure, confronts the project head-on, and emerges victorious. In the workplace, it's often the employees who take the initiative and embrace challenges that earn accolades and awards.

The concept extends beyond personal habits and professional challenges. It's a mindset that encompasses all facets of life. The most successful individuals in history are often distinguished by their ability to move beyond contemplation, to silence the avoider within, and to relentlessly pursue their goals. They transform thoughts into actions and challenges into opportunities.

In conclusion, the journcy from being a dreamer to becoming an action-taker requires a conscious shift in mindset. Realizing the distinction between envisioning change and actively working towards it is the key. By understanding that avoiding challenges is avoiding growth, and that awards often hide behind challenges, individuals can navigate from a passive contemplator to an empowered action-taker.

Consider the story of Maya, an aspiring entrepreneur. Fueled by a passion for her business idea, she spent months conceptualizing every detail. However, the real transformation occurred when Maya decided to take decisive steps toward making her vision a reality. She became an "Action-Taker." Instead of succumbing to the fear of failure or the comfort of endless planning, she initiated her business plan, reached out to potential partners, and embraced the challenges that came her way. In doing so, Maya not only brought her vision to life but also garnered the recognition and success she aspired to achieve.

The correlation between action-taking and self-belief is profound. The more an individual takes concrete steps toward their goals, the stronger their belief in their capabilities becomes. This cyclical process reinforces the idea that actions breed confidence, and confidence, in turn, fuels further action.

Let's delve into the realm of personal development. Imagine someone aspiring to become a proficient public speaker. The avoidance of this challenge might manifest in avoiding opportunities to speak publicly, rationalizing that it's beyond their abilities. On the contrary, the action-taker actively seeks speaking engagements, embraces the initial discomfort, and progressively refines their skills. Over time, they not only conquer the fear but also become adept at public speaking.

Consider the contrast between two individuals navigating the complexities of a career change. The avoider may perpetually contemplate the desire for change, listing reasons why it's impractical or risky. Meanwhile, the action-taker recognizes the need for a shift, updates their resume, networks, and actively pursues opportunities. The avoider remains in the realm of wishful thinking, while the action-taker transforms aspirations into a tangible career transition.

Practical implementation of this philosophy requires a fundamental shift in perspective. It involves asking oneself the crucial question: "When am I going to implement these thoughts into my life?" It's about setting realistic targets, breaking them into manageable steps, and progressively acting upon them. This approach extends beyond the personal sphere into the professional landscape, where individuals willing to take on challenges and turn them into opportunities often rise to leadership positions.

In essence, becoming an "Action-Taker and Avoider" is a choice that shapes not only the trajectory of one's personal and professional life but also influences the impact one can have on the world. It's a paradigm shift from passive contemplation to active engagement, from wishful thinking to purposeful action. The stories of those who have conquered challenges, embraced discomfort, and transformed their thoughts into actions serve as a testament to the transformative power of becoming an action-taker.

Consider the analogy of a budding artist who dreams of creating a masterpiece.

The avoider might spend hours contemplating the perfect brushstroke, the ideal color palette, and the flawless composition. Meanwhile, the action-taker, armed with imperfect strokes and a willingness to learn, sets out to paint. Through trial and error, learning from mistakes, and embracing the creative journey, they evolve from an avoider of the canvas to a true artist.

Now, let's shift our focus to the concept of avoiding Prakash, the challenges and awards that await in our endeavors. The avoider sees challenges as insurmountable obstacles, evading discomfort at all costs. In contrast, the action-taker views challenges as steppingstones to personal and professional growth. When faced with a daunting task, the action-taker understands that behind the challenge lies an opportunity to shine, learn, and achieve something extraordinary.

Consider the world of sports where athletes train rigorously, facing physical and mental challenges daily. The avoider might shy away from pushing their limits, fearing exhaustion or failure. On the flip side, the action-taker embraces the grueling workouts, understanding that each drop of sweat is a step closer to excellence. The eventual awards and victories are a direct result of confronting and conquering challenges head-on.

The dichotomy of action-taking and avoidance extends to decision-making. An avoider might procrastinate in making crucial decisions, fearing potential outcomes. Meanwhile, the action-taker recognizes that indecision is a decision in itself. They confront choices, weigh the options, and make informed decisions, thereby steering their life in the direction they desire.

In the narrative of life, each individual is the author of their story. The avoider might be content reading about the accomplishments of others, while the action-taker is busy writing their narrative. It's about recognizing that the pen is in your hand, and every action or inaction is a stroke on the canvas of your life.

Reflect on the story of Asha, who dreamed of contributing to social causes but remained an avoider for years. The turning point occurred when she actively volunteered at a local community center. The challenges were real, the efforts were tangible, and the impact was substantial. Asha transitioned from a passive well-wisher to an engaged contributor, illustrating that the greatest rewards lie on the other side of challenges.

In essence, the journey from avoider to action-taker is a profound transformation that shapes character, resilience, and success. It's about understanding that life's most significant achievements are often on the other side of discomfort and challenges. By actively participating in one's story, confronting challenges, and embracing opportunities, an individual becomes the protagonist of their narrative, steering it towards fulfillment and accomplishment.

As we navigate this exploration of becoming an action-taker and avoiding the comfort of inaction, remember that every action is a brushstroke, and every challenge is a canvas awaiting your masterpiece. The choice is yours — to merely envision greatness or to actively paint the strokes that lead to it.

In conclusion, the journey from being an avoider to becoming an action-taker is not merely a shift in mindset but a transformative voyage that shapes the very fabric of one's life. It is a conscious decision to move from passive contemplation to purposeful action, from wishful thinking to tangible implementation.

The stories of individuals who have embraced challenges, conquered discomfort, and turned their thoughts into actions serve as beacons of inspiration. Whether it's waking up early, pursuing a career change, or contributing to a greater cause, the underlying principle remains — the real magic happens when thoughts are translated into deeds.

Avoiding Prakash, the challenges and awards that await us, might seem like a comforting choice, but it's the action-taker who understands that growth lies beyond the veil of comfort. Challenges are not roadblocks but steppingstones to personal and professional elevation.

As you embark on your own narrative, recognize that the pen is in your hands. Each action you take, every challenge you confront, contributes to the canvas of your life. It's a canvas awaiting the strokes of your aspirations, the colors of your efforts, and the masterpiece of your achievements.

In the grand tapestry of life, being an action-taker is not just a choice; it's a commitment to living authentically, facing challenges courageously, and scripting a story worth telling. The awards, the victories, and the fulfillment of your deepest aspirations await on the path where you cease to be an avoider and become the protagonist of your journey.

So, dare to dream, but more importantly, dare to act. The true essence of life unfolds not in contemplation but in the bold strokes of action. Embrace challenges, pursue your goals, and watch as your narrative transforms into a compelling tale of resilience, growth, and triumph. In the end, it's not about avoiding discomfort; it's about thriving in the face of it, emerging as the artist and storyteller of your extraordinary life."

The Secret Power of Imagination & Affirmation: The Art and Science of Manifesting Your Dreams

"Vision Boards: Your Gateway to Imagination Formation"

Embark on a transformative journey into the profound realm of imagination formation. While countless books touch upon harnessing the power of imagination, today, we'll delve into its practical essence, understanding its significance through motivation and real-world examples. The challenge often lies not in understanding these known secrets but in their application. Imagination formation emerges as a significant yet underutilized key in this process, capable of unlocking unprecedented potentials.

As you commit to the pages of this book, poised for the transformation of your life, discard the crutch of logical reasoning and immerse yourself in practical application. The wisdom shared here transcends the theoretical, finding resonance in the very fabric of your existence.

Picture this journey as a tapestry woven with threads of positive attitude and self-belief. The seeds planted at the beginning of this book now sprout into a garden of possibilities. Just as your faith in an unseen higher power remains unwavering, infuse that same belief into your dreams and visions. This robust belief serves as a shield, an armor protecting your aspirations from doubt and skepticism.

Consider the illustrious journey of Oprah Winfrey, a living testament to the transformative power of imagination. Born into adversity, she imagined a life beyond her circumstances and manifested her dreams into a reality that transcends borders. Her story resonates with the principles we explore here — the power of envisioning a reality different from the present.

Through consistent day-and-night imagination, witness the seamless alignment of circumstances. Imagination formation is not just about envisioning; it is a dance with gratitude and a deep sense of deservingness. As the great Helen Keller once said, "The only thing worse than being blind is having sight but no vision." Your vision, fueled by imagination, propels you forward.

The Law of Attraction steps into this narrative, not as a mere concept but as a force of nature. As the acclaimed motivational speaker Tony Robbins puts it, "Whatever you hold in your mind on a consistent basis is exactly what you will experience in your life." Understand that everything shared in this book gains significance through practical application.

Celebrities discreetly leverage this secret, often termed the Power of the Subconscious Mind. Jim Carrey, before becoming a Hollywood sensation, wrote himself a check for $10 million, dated it for 10 years in the future, and visualized himself receiving it. His unwavering belief in his imaginative vision led him to manifest that exact amount with the movie "Dumb and Dumber."

Imagine a world where everyone comprehends and implements these principles – a world abundant with successful individuals. The wisdom shared here is not just a collection of ideas; it's a call to action. It's a summons to recognize that you're on a path of achievement, prepared for unconventional endeavors. Distill the essence from countless books, quotes, and examples — it all converges into one core concept: imagination.

Commence and conclude each day with imaginative practices, for as Albert Einstein asserted, "Imagination is more important than knowledge. For knowledge is limited, whereas imagination embraces the entire world, stimulating progress, giving birth to evolution." Your journey unfolds with the transformative Power of Imagination, a beacon of hope guiding you towards the life you envision.

Real-Life Examples of Imagination's Triumph

Oprah Winfrey: From Adversity to Global Influence

Oprah Winfrey's life story exemplifies the transformative power of imagination. Born into adversity, she envisioned a life far beyond her challenging circumstances. Through unwavering belief and consistent imagination, Oprah turned her dreams into a reality that transcended borders. Her journey serves as a testament to the profound impact of envisioning a reality different from the present.

Jim Carrey: Manifesting $10 Million with Imagination

Before Jim Carrey became a Hollywood sensation, he harnessed the Power of the Subconscious Mind through imagination. Carrey wrote himself a check for $10 million, dated it for 10 years in the future, and visualized himself receiving it. His steadfast belief in this imaginative vision led to the manifestation of that exact amount through the success of the movie "Dumb and Dumber." Carrey's story highlights the tangible results that can emerge from dedicated imagination formation.

Tony Robbins: The Law of Attraction in Action

Tony Robbins, a renowned motivational speaker, emphasizes the practical application of the Law of Attraction. According to Robbins, "Whatever you hold in your mind on a consistent basis is exactly what you will experience in your life." This principle underscores the significance of maintaining a positive and focused imagination to attract corresponding manifestations into one's life. Robbins's teachings provide a roadmap for individuals to leverage the Law of Attraction for their personal and professional growth.

Sachin Tendulkar and Virat Kohli: Imagination in Sports Excellence

The Power of Imagination is not limited to the realm of entertainment; it extends to sports excellence. Cricket legends Sachin Tendulkar and Virat Kohli showcase the impact of imagination on their performance. Beyond talent and hard work, their ability to tap into the power of their subconscious minds through imagination contributes to their success. Whether visualizing a successful inning or envisioning victory, these athletes demonstrate the transformative potential of harnessing the imagination in the world of sports.

Albert Einstein: Imagination as the Source of Progress

Albert Einstein's profound insight, "Imagination is more important than knowledge," underscores the foundational role imagination plays in human progress. Einstein recognized that knowledge has limits, but imagination has the power to embrace the entire world, stimulating progress and giving birth to evolution. His perspective reinforces the idea that true advancements originate from the imaginative realm. In the context of personal transformation, embracing Einstein's wisdom becomes a key to unlocking limitless possibilities.

Vision Boards: A Dynamic Tool for Imagination Formation

Within the pages of this narrative, I've articulated the transformative concept of Imagination Formation. The term "Formation" has likely crossed your path in diverse literature, manifesting in various contexts. Picture, if you will, a canvas of dreams known as the vision board – more than a mere collage, it's a tool of manifestation. It involves placing your aspirations, like "Successful Writer, Best-selling Author," alongside a set date. This seemingly simple act initiates a powerful process – Formation.

Let's dive deeper into the enchanting realm of vision boards. They are akin to creating a visual roadmap for your aspirations. Imagine a budding author fervently visualizing their name on the "New York Times Bestseller" list. This act serves as a catalyst, a constant reminder of the path they aspire to tread.

As you stand at the crossroads of imagination and formation, envision this captivating process unfolding. Consider an artist painting a masterpiece without first envisioning it in their mind. Your life's masterpiece begins with the vivid strokes of imagination. Moments of tension may arise, and you might falter in your commitment to daily visualization. Yet, the vision board stands as your unwavering ally, drawing you back into the realm of your aspirations.

Reflect on the tale of a struggling entrepreneur maintaining a vision board adorned with symbols of success despite setbacks. Night after night, they immerse themselves in the mental imagery of achieving their goals, expressing gratitude for the journey.

The magic lies in the synergy of Imagination and Formation – an alchemy that transforms desires into tangible realities. Picture a musician composing a symphony; the melody originates in the composer's mind, a product of vivid imagination. Apply this principle to your life's symphony – imagine it, compose it, and witness it unfold.

As you pen down your dreams with your own handwriting, you infuse them with a personal touch. Imagine an architect sketching the blueprint of a magnificent structure; your handwritten aspirations are the architectural plans for your future.

In life's grand tapestry, the vision board serves as a thread connecting you to your dreams. It's not just wishful thinking; it's a dynamic process that, when coupled with unwavering belief, turns the perceived impossible into the achievable.

So, immerse yourself in the art of Imagination and Formation. Let your vision board be a living, breathing entity guiding your journey. Combine the elements like a maestro orchestrating a symphony, and watch miracles unfold in your life. Thank you for joining this transformative exploration.

Discovering the Magic: How the Law of Attraction Works

Let's uncover the secrets behind the intriguing concept known as the law of attraction. Imagine it as a powerful force, similar to gravity, weaving through our lives. This cosmic phenomenon, discussed in various ways, is like gravity but influences the energy and thoughts we send out.

Think of the universe as a giant web of energy, where each of us adds to a shared pool. Whether you see this as a higher power or just a shared energy, the idea is potent. When someone leaves, their energy spreads, leaving a lasting impact — a reminder that we're fundamentally beings of energy.

Now, think about tuning into frequencies. Each of us has a unique frequency that affects our feelings, thoughts, and experiences. The law of attraction suggests that aligning our frequency with what we want attracts similar energies from the universe.

Consider the power of positive thinking and visualization. Have you ever had sudden bursts of creativity or groundbreaking ideas seemingly out of nowhere? It's like you tapped into a frequency that was once hard to reach. This is the enchantment of life attraction. By regularly visualizing your goals, you tune into the frequency associated with those dreams.

Imagine it like tuning a radio; to hear classical music, you tune to the classical frequency. Similarly, aligning your energy with positive thoughts and goals tunes you into the frequency that attracts those things. The universe responds to your tuned frequency, bringing ideas, opportunities, and experiences aligned with your desires.

Successful people often credit the law of attraction for their achievements. Entrepreneurs, artists, and visionaries talk about how staying positive and picturing success played a crucial role. Take Steve Jobs, who said, "Your work is going to fill a large part of your life, and the only way to be truly satisfied is to do what you believe is great work."

To sum up, the mystery of life attraction revolves around the idea that our thoughts and energies create a connection with the universe. By understanding and embracing this concept, we open ourselves to a world of possibilities aligned with our frequency. Stay positive, be committed to your dreams, and see the magic of life attraction unfold in your journey.

Now, let's go even deeper into how life attraction works. Picture your thoughts and emotions as vibrations spreading through the universe. The law of attraction suggests that like attracts like; focusing on positive thoughts draws corresponding positive energies.

Think about "after energy." When we talk or express thoughts, we emit energy into the universe. Whether acknowledging a higher power or recognizing our connection, our shared energy forms a strong force.

Consider spiritual practices focusing on connecting with supreme energy. It's about aligning not just with individual frequencies but with the grand symphony of the universe. This alignment propels us forward, creating a harmonious flow of energy between us and the cosmos.

As we go through life, moments of inspiration are not coincidences but reflections of our connection to particular frequencies. Think of the solar energy analogy; each form of energy has a unique frequency, and our thoughts and emotions emit frequencies resonating with corresponding energies in the universe.

Recall times when ideas flowed effortlessly or you felt a deep connection to a situation. These moments are about aligning your frequency with the vast energy field of the universe, not just chance.

Now, let's explore the power of imagination and formation. Visualization is a strong tool in the law of attraction. Creating a mental image of your desired outcome helps connect with the associated frequency. Here, imagination and formation come together to shape your reality.

Think of successful athletes who visualize victories before they happen. By envisioning success, they tune into the frequency of achievement, boosting their performance. It shows how our thoughts influence our actions and reality.

In essence, the law of attraction encourages us to be intentional creators of our experiences. By understanding energy frequencies, positive thinking, and visualization, we unlock a realm where our dreams become real. It's not just wishful thinking; it's a conscious alignment with the energies shaping our existence.

As you navigate life, remember your power to shape reality. Embrace frequencies that align with your dreams, stay tuned to the universe's symphony, and witness the magic of life attraction in every part of your journey.

Now, let's bring these concepts to life with some real examples.

Example 1: The Positive Spiral

Imagine waking up feeling grumpy, thinking the day will be terrible. You're emitting negative energy. As a result, you might notice more things going wrong — spilled coffee, a traffic jam. Your negative energy attracts more negative experiences.

Now, picture waking up with a positive mindset. You expect a good day, and suddenly, you find a parking spot right away or receive a compliment. Your positive energy attracts positive experiences.

Example 2: The Job Seeker's Journey

Consider two job seekers with similar skills. One is always worried about not finding a job, emitting anxious energy. The other stays positive, believing the right opportunity will come. The positive thinker may network better, find more opportunities, and eventually land the job because their energy aligns with success.

Example 3: The Dream Home Vision

Let's say you dream of owning a beautiful house. Regularly visualizing it, feeling the joy of living there, aligns your encrgy with that dream. You may start noticing opportunities to save money or find the perfect home because your thoughts have tuned you into the frequency of achieving that goal.

The Power of "Self Realization"

A Journey into Self-Discovery

Exploring the profound concept of "Self-Realization," or "Aatm Manthan" in Hindi, is like embarking on a transformative odyssey into understanding oneself. It's not just important but a key to sustaining success. In moments when thoughts of quitting threaten to invade our minds, reflecting on the spark that initiated this journey becomes crucial.

**Initiating Your Journey: **

Every pursuit begins with a thought, a vision, and a belief in oneself. Remind yourself that you are the author of this journey, holding the reins to its outcome.

**Practice of Self-Realization: **

Dedicating time for self-reflection involves contemplating, asking questions, and finding answers from within. Channeling thoughts towards self-belief, confidence, and positivity paves the way for a clear and purposeful path.

**15-20 Minutes a Day: **

In today's fast-paced life, even allocating 15 to 20 minutes each day, especially in the morning, can yield remarkable results.

The Importance of Visualization and Imagination

Navigating Life's Challenges:

Visualizing your path, contemplating your journey, and strategizing how to overcome obstacles are integral to self-realization. This internal dialogue becomes a compass, guiding you towards your desired destination.

You are the Author:

Remind yourself that you are the author of your story, and self-realization is the tool that empowers you to script a narrative aligned with your aspirations. It's about cultivating permanent motivation from within.

Self-Realization in Perseverance and Success 

🚀 **Foundation of Mandated Success: **

While external motivational content provides a temporary boost, permanent motivation comes from within. Self-realization becomes the foundation of mandated success.

 **The Journey's Triumph: **

Consider it an opportunity to achieve true success rooted in a deep understanding of yourself. Let self-realization be the guiding force that fuels your determination, perseverance, and ultimate triumph.

Unveiling the Depths of Personal Triumph 🎲

The notion of the "Power of Self-Realization," or "Aatm Manthan," delves into the profound journey of introspection and self-discovery. It's not just a choice but a necessity for sustaining and achieving enduring success.

🚀 **Ritu's Entrepreneurial Success: **

Consider the story of Ritu, an aspiring entrepreneur facing numerous challenges. In moments of self-doubt, her engagement in self-realization, reflecting on her passion for innovation and a desire to make a positive impact, became the driving force behind her perseverance and the success of her venture.

A Journey into the Inner Landscape 🗺️

Self-realization is not a fleeting moment of motivation but an ongoing dialogue with oneself. In the midst of life's chaos, dedicating even a brief period each day to self-reflection can unravel profound insights.

🛩️ **Arjun's Professional Evolution: **

Meet Arjun, a professional navigating the complexities of a competitive career. In his daily practice of self-realization, visualizing his trajectory and addressing challenges transform his mindset, fostering resilience and strategic thinking.

The Visualization and Imagination Nexus

Visualizing the journey and imagining desired outcomes are intrinsic to self-realization. Picture Meera, an aspiring artist, and Kavya, a student with ambitious career goals, as they employ the power of visualization to shape their destinies.

**Meera's Artistic Journey: **

Meera immerses herself in the creative process, evolving from a contemplator to a true artist through trial, error, and embracing the journey.

**Kavya's Academic Vision: **

Through self-realization, Kavya identifies motivations, confronts self-doubt, and envisions achieving academic excellence, making her mental imagery a guiding light.

Catalyst for Perseverance and True Success

In the realm of perseverance, external motivation serves as a fleeting spark, while self-realization becomes the enduring flame.

🏆 **Vikram's Athletic Triumph: **

Vikram, an athlete facing setbacks, engaged in self-realization, introspecting on his commitment to the sport, his love for competition, and his vision of success. This intrinsic motivation became the bedrock of his resilience, leading to unparalleled athletic achievements.

**Anaya's Professional Transformation: **

Anaya, a professional seeking career growth, transforms into a strategic, empowered professional through consistent self-reflection.

The Mandate for Achieving Sustained Success 🌐

In conclusion, self-realization is not merely a concept but a mandate for achieving sustained success. Through engaging stories, we witness the transformative power of understanding oneself.

Orchestrating Your Symphony of Success:

In the grand narrative of life, make self-realization a compass guiding you through challenges and triumphs. It is the unwavering belief in your journey, the visualization of your destination, and the commitment to your aspirations that define the essence of the "Power of Self-Realization."

The Enchantment of Life's Essence: A Deep Dive into Love, Affection, and Gratitude

In the intricate fabric of existence, we discover the profound influence of three seemingly simple yet remarkably potent words – Love, Affection, and Gratitude. These aren't just verbal expressions; they are transformative forces, guiding lights that illuminate the path to greatness in our journey through life.

What's truly enchanting is that these treasures are bestowed upon us without a price tag, free of charge. Let's embark on an immersive exploration into the mystical realm of Love, Affection, and Gratitude, unraveling the magic they can weave into the very fabric of our lives. 🚀

Beyond the surface utterance of these words lies a deeper understanding of their significance. Love, Affection, and Gratitude aren't mere concepts; they emerge as sturdy pillars, fortifying our journey and providing resilience to navigate the intricacies of life. 🌀 These treasures are not commodities that can be purchased; rather, they are bestowed upon us as priceless gifts.

These words, far from being abstract, are actionable principles that actively mold our destiny. Expressing gratitude for both divine blessings and our own accomplishments becomes the key to unlocking a life brimming with abundance. The futility of perpetual complaints is illuminated – an individual perpetually complaining finds themselves ensnared in a cycle of negativity. ☹

Consider the moments of dissatisfaction when you wished for more yesterday. Has today not mirrored the same pattern? Breaking free from this cycle entails embracing an attitude of acceptance, acknowledging and expressing sincere thanks for the present, and then shifting focus to the future. Those who adopt this mindset find themselves lacking nothing; their positive attitude becomes a magnetic force attracting further blessings. 🔄

The intricate connection between attitude and abundance extends beyond material possessions; it is a universal law encompassing knowledge, goals, and dreams. The emphasis lies not only on harboring dreams but cultivating a deep and abiding love for them, as without love and affection, the magnetic force of attraction remains elusive. 🩶

The essence of this chapter lies in the exploration of how attitude acts as the driving force, shaping our perspectives and influencing the outcomes we attract. It is an invitation to internalize this understanding, to integrate this attitude into the very core of our being.

The narrative seamlessly weaves together elements of gratitude, love, and attitude, creating an intricate tapestry of interconnected principles. It serves as a guide, encouraging readers to utilize these three magical words as transformative tools for a fulfilling life.

Let's delve into a scenario where you harbor a dream or goal. Recognize the pivotal role that love and affection play in realizing that dream. Without a deep-seated love for our aspirations, the magnetic force that attracts success remains dormant. This is a call to action, a reminder that achieving significant milestones requires not just effort but a genuine emotional investment.

As we navigate through the pages of this chapter, let's contemplate the interconnectedness of these principles. The tapestry of our lives is woven with threads of love, affection, and gratitude, intricately linked to the attitude we choose to adopt. It's a reminder that every aspect of our journey, whether acquiring knowledge or pursuing aspirations, is influenced by our attitude.

The narrative takes a tangible turn with real-life examples, illustrating the significance of expressing gratitude in everyday encounters. Imagine standing at the crossroads of dissatisfaction and contentment. The beggar, devoid of hands and legs, yearns for life, serving as a poignant reminder of the resilience within us. On the flip side, those overcoming physical challenges through hard work exemplify the power of a positive mindset. It prompts reflection on our own blessings, fostering a deep sense of gratitude for the gift of a healthy body and the ability to work.

Introducing a spiritual dimension, readers are encouraged to express gratitude sincerely to the higher power. The authenticity of this appreciation is emphasized; it's not a mere recitation of words but a genuine outpouring of thanks for every facet of life – family, children, professional endeavors.

This practice, when directed towards the higher power, becomes a conduit for more blessings, echoing the universal truth that the more gratitude expressed, the more one receives.

Transitioning into the power of attraction, readers are urged to visualize their desires with love and affection. The analogy of upgrading from a Honda City to a Mercedes becomes a metaphor for life's aspirations. It's not about diminishing the value of what one has but appreciating it while aspiring for more. The emphasis is on staying positive, acknowledging others' successes without harboring negativity, and channeling that energy into personal growth.

The narrative takes a philosophical turn, emphasizing the importance of time as a valuable currency. Its wise utilization is pivotal in attracting abundance effortlessly. The central message is clear - time is more precious than money. By valuing time, making oneself invaluable, and aligning with positive energies, one can attract success in various forms.

This chapter unfolds as a tapestry woven with the threads of love, affection, and gratitude, intricately tied together by the attitude one chooses to embrace. It's a journey of self-discovery and empowerment, urging readers to internalize these principles and embark on a path towards positive transformation. As the chapter concludes, it's not just an end but a continuation of these magical words into every facet of one's life, creating a symphony of love, affection, and gratitude that resonates not only in one's heart but with the universe. Thank you for your continued engagement in this transformative exploration.

Acknowledging a fundamental truth – time is the great equalizer. Everyone possesses the same amount of time. Utilizing this precious resource wisely is implored. Employing imagination, the power affirmation, love, affection, and positive attitude as tools to create shortcuts and accelerate progress is encouraged. Regardless of the quantity of resources at one's disposal, cultivating a perpetual state of happiness is underscored. Love, affection, and attitude, when embedded in every aspect of life, become catalysts for positive transformation.

Expanding the narrative to a sacred space – the moments of quiet reflection in front of God. Here, a profound practice is introduced – expressing thanks from the heart. Gratitude becomes a spiritual bridge, connecting one to the divine. It's not just a recitation of words; it's a genuine outpouring of thanks for every facet of life – family, children, professional endeavors. Readers are urged to express heartfelt gratitude to everyone who has made a positive impact on their lives.

This practice, it is contended, has the potential to bring about life-altering changes, so impactful that finding the right words to express it becomes a challenge. In this exploration of life's magical words – Love, Affection, and Gratitude – the transformative power of gratitude emerges as a recurring theme.

In conclusion, readers are reinforced with the importance of cultivating a positive attitude for everything in their lives. The habit of expressing thanks becomes a cornerstone of this attitude. The authenticity of expression is underscored – it's not about words from the mouth but emanating from the heart. Connecting this back to the magnetic nature of love and affection, expressing love for something attracts similar energies.

A powerful analogy is presented – envisioning a dream car parked in front of one's house. To make it theirs, showing genuine affection and love for it, coupled with the right emotions, thoughts, and positive attitude. The message is clear: what one expresses love and gratitude towards, one attracts into their life.

As this chapter comes to a close, a sincere thank you is extended for the patience in reading. The hope is that this exploration has sparked a positive change in readers' lives. Let's step into the next chapter with renewed enthusiasm, armed with the magical words that can shape destinies. Thank you for joining in this transformative journey.

"Be Your Own Mentor: Igniting Self-Motivation"

In this profound exploration of self-motivation, we delve into the captivating journey of becoming your own mentor, igniting the transformative force within. Recognizing the limitations of relying solely on external motivation becomes the catalyst for self-discovery and sustained internal inspiration. As we navigate through each chapter, we unravel the intricacies of awakening the teacher within, creating a harmonious symphony of success and fulfillment.

Chapter 1: Internalizing Motivation - The Need for Self-Reliance

Our journey begins with a fundamental understanding of the necessity to internalize motivation. The ephemeral nature of relying on external factors necessitates a shift towards cultivating an internal source. We embark on a thoughtful exploration of the limitations of depending on others for motivation, setting the stage for a profound journey within.

In today's fast-paced world, where external stimuli abound, it becomes imperative to anchor ourselves in the understanding that true motivation springs from within. Relying solely on external validation can lead to a fragile foundation for our aspirations. As we internalize the need for self-reliance in motivation, we lay the groundwork for a resilient and enduring source of inspiration.

Chapter 2: Discovering the Inherent Teacher - Recognizing Your Motivational Mentor

Every individual possesses an inherent teacher, a motivational mentor awaiting recognition. Unveiling the characteristics of this internal guide becomes paramount for sustained self-motivation. Through introspective exercises and reflections, we guide readers to identify and acknowledge the presence of this intrinsic mentor.

Imagine this mentor as a guiding light within, a source of wisdom attuned to your values and aspirations. This chapter delves into the intricacies of recognizing and understanding the motivational mentor within, emphasizing its role in shaping a purpose-driven life. Real-life anecdotes illuminate the transformative power of acknowledging and embracing this inherent teacher.

Chapter 3: The Power of Consistency - Nurturing Your Internal Motivator

Consistency emerges as a cornerstone in nurturing the internal motivator. Delving into the art of cultivating a consistent relationship with this mentor within, we explore strategies to ensure a reliable source of guidance and encouragement. Through practical insights and actionable steps, readers are equipped to establish a steadfast connection with their internal motivator.

Consistency is not merely a routine but a conscious choice to align actions with aspirations consistently.

This chapter provides a roadmap for individuals to forge a lasting bond with their motivational mentor, fostering an environment where inspiration becomes a constant companion on the journey to success.

Chapter 4: Breaking Dependency - Transitioning to Self-Motivation

Shifting from dependency on external motivators to self-motivation requires a conscious effort. This transformative chapter delves into practical tips and real-life examples, guiding individuals through the process of breaking free from the shackles of dependence. Through inspiring narratives and actionable steps, readers are empowered to take control of their motivational journey.

Dependency on external validation often creates a fragile foundation, susceptible to external fluctuations. As we explore the nuances of transitioning to self-motivation, readers are encouraged to embark on a journey of self-discovery, realizing the untapped reservoir of strength and inspiration within.

Chapter 5: Unleashing the Potential - How Your Internal Mentor Guides You

The potential within, guided by the internal mentor, holds the key to unlocking unprecedented success. This chapter delves into real-life scenarios where individuals harnessed their internal motivational force to achieve remarkable feats. Emphasizing the limitless possibilities, we showcase the transformative power of unleashing one's potential under the guidance of the internal mentor.

Real-world examples narrate tales of individuals who, by awakening their internal mentor, have defied conventional limitations and achieved extraordinary milestones. Through these narratives, readers gain insights into the profound impact of aligning actions with the inherent guidance that resides within.

Chapter 6: Sustaining Motivation - Strategies for Long-Term Self-Motivation

Maintaining motivation over the long term requires a strategic approach. This comprehensive chapter offers practical insights and actionable steps to empower individuals in sustaining self-motivation, even in the face of challenges. By addressing the common pitfalls and providing effective strategies, readers are equipped with the tools needed for enduring inspiration.

Motivation is not a fleeting emotion but a sustainable force that propels individuals towards their goals. Through the lens of long-term self-motivation, readers learn to navigate the ebb and flow of life while staying committed to their aspirations.

Chapter 7: Integrating Lessons - Applying Internal Guidance to Daily Life

Applying the lessons learned from the internal mentor to everyday life is essential. This chapter focuses on integrating the guidance received into daily practices, ensuring a seamless alignment of internal motivation with external actions. Through practical scenarios and relatable examples, readers gain insights into making self-motivation a lived experience.

The true test of self-motivation lies in its integration into the fabric of daily routines. As readers learn to apply internal guidance to real-life situations, they witness the transformative power of aligning actions with the inherent wisdom residing within.

Chapter 8: Inspiring Others - Becoming a Source of Motivation

The journey within not only transforms individuals but also equips them to inspire others. This chapter delves into understanding how self-motivation can radiate positive influence, creating a ripple effect in motivating those around you. Through real-world examples, readers witness the transformative impact of becoming a source of motivation for others.

Inspiration, when shared, multiplies in its potency. As individuals embrace their role as motivators, they contribute to a positive and uplifting environment, fostering a community driven by shared aspirations and collective growth.

Chapter 9: The Art of Reflection - Harnessing the Wisdom Within

In this reflective chapter, we explore the art of reflection as a powerful tool for self-discovery and motivation. Taking time to reflect on one's actions, thoughts, and decisions enables individuals to tap into the reservoir of wisdom within. Through various reflection techniques and practices, readers learn to enhance their connection with the internal mentor, fostering self-awareness and personal growth.

Reflection is not a passive activity but an intentional practice that deepens the understanding of one's motivations and aspirations. As readers engage in the art of reflection, they uncover new layers of self-awareness, contributing to a more profound connection with their internal mentor.

Chapter 10: Embracing Vulnerability - A Catalyst for Inner Transformation

Embracing vulnerability becomes a transformative catalyst on the journey to self-motivation. This chapter discusses the significance of acknowledging vulnerabilities, understanding their role in personal development, and leveraging them as steppingstones towards unleashing inner strength. Real-life stories exemplify how vulnerability, when embraced, becomes a powerful force in self-motivation.

Vulnerability is not a weakness but a reservoir of strength waiting to be tapped. Through personal narratives and relatable examples, readers are encouraged to embrace their vulnerabilities as integral components of their journey towards self-discovery and sustained motivation.

Chapter 11: Building a Supportive Environment - Surrounding Yourself with Positivity

Creating a supportive environment is crucial for sustaining self-motivation. This chapter explores the impact of external influences on internal motivation and provides insights into curating positive and encouraging surroundings. Practical tips and examples demonstrate how individuals can actively shape their environment to align with their motivational goals.

The external environment plays a significant role in either nurturing or hindering self-motivation. As readers

 understand the dynamics of building a supportive ecosystem, they gain the tools to proactively shape their surroundings, fostering an environment conducive to personal growth and success.

Chapter 12: Cultivating a Growth Mindset - Nurturing a Positive Perspective

Cultivating a growth mindset becomes instrumental in sustaining self-motivation. This chapter delves into the concept of a growth mindset, exploring how adopting a positive perspective towards challenges and setbacks fuels internal motivation. Through actionable strategies and real-life examples, readers learn to cultivate a mindset that embraces continuous learning and resilience.

A growth mindset perceives challenges as opportunities for growth, setbacks as steppingstones towards success. As readers immerse themselves in the principles of cultivating a growth mindset, they witness a transformative shift in their approach to obstacles, fostering a resilient and motivated mindset.

Chapter 13: Aligning Values with Actions - A Blueprint for Authentic Motivation

Aligning values with actions becomes a blueprint for authentic motivation. This chapter examines the profound impact of living in alignment with one's core values on sustained self-motivation. Through introspective exercises and illustrative examples, readers discover the transformative power of authenticity in motivation.

Values serve as a compass, guiding individuals towards a purposeful and meaningful life. As readers delve into the process of aligning values with actions, they unlock the door to authentic motivation, where every action resonates with the core principles that define their unique journey.

Chapter 14: The Rituals of Renewal - Nourishing Your Motivational Spirit

In this chapter, we explore the significance of rituals as powerful tools for renewing and nourishing the motivational spirit. Establishing rituals that align with personal aspirations and values becomes a cornerstone for sustained self-motivation. Practical insights and examples guide readers in creating rituals that foster a continual sense of renewal.

Rituals are not mere routines but intentional acts that replenish the motivational reservoir. As readers integrate the concept of rituals into their lives, they discover a source of consistent inspiration that transcends the challenges of daily life, ensuring a continual sense of renewal on their motivational journey.

Chapter 15: The Dance of Discipline and Freedom - Balancing Commitment and Flexibility

Balancing discipline and freedom is pivotal in sustaining self-motivation. This chapter explores the delicate dance between commitment and flexibility, emphasizing the importance of discipline in achieving goals while allowing for adaptability in the face of change. Real-life stories illustrate the transformative impact of finding the equilibrium between these two forces.

Discipline provides the structure needed for sustained motivation, while flexibility allows for creative adaptation to unforeseen circumstances. As readers navigate the dance of discipline and freedom, they acquire the skills to maintain a harmonious balance, ensuring resilience and commitment on their motivational journey.

Chapter 16: Embodying Gratitude - A Catalyst for Motivational Alchemy

Gratitude emerges as a potent catalyst for motivational alchemy. This chapter delves into the transformative power of cultivating gratitude as a means to amplify self-motivation. Through practical exercises and real-life examples, readers learn to harness the alchemical effects of gratitude in fostering a positive and motivated mindset.

Gratitude is not just an emotion but a practice that enhances the perception of one's blessings. As readers embody gratitude in their daily lives, they witness the alchemy that occurs, turning challenges into opportunities and setbacks into steppingstones on the path to sustained motivation.

Chapter 17: The Symphony of Self-Care - Nurturing Mind, Body, and Soul

Self-care becomes the symphony that nurtures the mind, body, and soul. This chapter explores the holistic approach to self-care as an integral component of sustained self-motivation. Practical tips and illustrative examples guide readers in creating a harmonious self-care routine that supports their motivational journey.

The symphony of self-care encompasses physical, mental, and emotional well-being. As readers understand the interconnectedness of self-care and self-motivation, they cultivate a holistic approach that ensures a thriving and resilient foundation for their journey towards success and fulfillment.

Chapter 18: Embracing Setbacks - Lessons in Resilience and Adaptability

Embracing setbacks becomes a masterclass in resilience and adaptability on the self-motivation journey. This chapter explores the transformative potential of setbacks, reframing them as valuable lessons rather than obstacles. Real-life stories of individuals overcoming adversity serve as beacons of inspiration for readers facing their own challenges.

Setbacks are not roadblocks but detours leading to unforeseen opportunities. As readers internalize the art of embracing setbacks, they develop resilience and adaptability, essential qualities that fortify their motivational spirit in the face of adversity.

Chapter 19: Radiating Motivation Across Your Sphere

Self-motivation extends its influence beyond individual accomplishments, creating a ripple effect in one's sphere of influence. This chapter explores how individuals, driven by self-motivation, become catalysts for positive change in their communities, workplaces, and relationships. Real-world examples illustrate the profound impact of spreading motivation to inspire collective growth.

The journey of self-motivation is not solitary but radiates outward, touching the lives of those within one's sphere. As readers understand their potential to influence and inspire others, they become active participants in a collective journey towards growth, positivity, and shared success.

Chapter 20: Evolving with Purpose - Navigating the Journey Beyond

As individuals progress on their self-motivation journey, they evolve with purpose. This final chapter explores the continuous evolution fueled by self-motivation, emphasizing the dynamic nature of personal growth. Insights from thought leaders, combined with personal narratives, provide a comprehensive perspective on navigating the journey beyond initial self-discovery.

The journey of self-motivation is an ever-evolving expedition, marked by continuous growth and purposeful evolution. As readers embrace the concept of evolving with purpose, they become architects of their destiny, navigating the uncharted territories of personal development with resilience, enthusiasm, and a deep sense of purpose.

Chapter 21: The Art of Celebration - Acknowledging Milestones on the Journey

Celebration becomes an art form on the journey of self-motivation. This additional chapter explores the significance of acknowledging and celebrating milestones, no matter how small. Through practical suggestions and real-life anecdotes, readers learn to infuse joy and gratitude into their ongoing journey, reinforcing the positive cycle of motivation.

Celebration is not just a reward for achievements but a catalyst for continued motivation. As readers embrace the art of celebration, they cultivate a mindset that appreciates progress, fostering a sense of fulfillment that propels them forward on their self-motivation journey.

Chapter 22: The Wisdom of Adaptability - Navigating Change with Grace

Adaptability becomes a vital component of sustained self-motivation, especially in the face of change. This chapter delves into the wisdom of adaptability, offering insights and strategies for navigating transitions with grace. Real-life examples showcase individuals who embraced change as an opportunity for growth, inspiring readers to cultivate a flexible mindset.

Change is inevitable, and adaptability is the key to thriving amidst uncertainty. As readers explore the wisdom of adaptability, they develop the resilience needed to navigate the ever-changing landscape of life, ensuring that external shifts become opportunities for continued self-motivation.

Chapter 23: The Collaborative Symphony - Cultivating Motivational Partnerships

Collaboration and shared motivation amplify individual efforts. This chapter explores the concept of collaborative motivation, emphasizing the transformative power of partnerships. Through case studies and practical advice, readers gain insights into how motivational alliances can enhance personal growth and collective success.

Motivational partnerships provide mutual support and encouragement, creating a synergistic effect. As readers learn to cultivate collaborative symphonies, they contribute to a dynamic and uplifting community where individuals inspire and uplift each other on their respective journeys of self-motivation.

Chapter 24: Legacy of Motivation - Crafting a Lasting Impact

The final addition to this symphony explores the concept of leaving a legacy of motivation. Individuals driven by self-motivation have the potential to create a lasting impact on future generations. Through inspirational stories and reflective exercises, readers are prompted to consider the legacy they wish to leave and how their journey can inspire those who follow.

The legacy of motivation extends beyond individual achievements, becoming a beacon for others to follow. As readers contemplate the imprint they want to make, they realize the profound impact their commitment to self-motivation can have on shaping a positive and empowered future.

Conclusion: A Lifelong Symphony of Self-Motivation - Your Ongoing Journey

As we conclude this extensive exploration into the realm of self-motivation, it becomes evident that this journey is a lifelong symphony. The internal mentor, awakened and nurtured throughout this book, becomes an enduring companion. This is not merely a guide to self-motivation; it's an invitation to embark on a continuous, transformative journey.

The chapters have unfolded a roadmap, guiding you to be your own mentor, to awaken the teacher within, and to let self-motivation orchestrate a symphony of success and fulfillment in your life. The insights, strategies, and real-life examples provided are not just tools; they are notes in your personal symphony.

Each chapter, a crescendo of wisdom; each lesson, a harmonious melody. Your journey doesn't end with the last page; it evolves into a continuous, purposeful rhythm. The internal mentor, now a constant presence, continues to guide, inspire, and empower, ensuring a life that resonates with purpose and self-motivation.

In essence, this book serves as a symphony conductor's wand, empowering you to lead the orchestra of your life. The melodies of self-motivation harmonize with the rhythm of your actions, creating a beautiful composition of success, fulfillment, and personal growth.

As you embark on this ongoing journey of self-motivation, may your symphony be grand, and may the echoes of your internal mentor reverberate through every aspect of your life. Thank you for being part of this transformative experience. The curtain may ...fall on this book, but the symphony of self-motivation within you is poised for a timeless encore.

Final Thoughts: Your Symphony, Your Legacy

As we conclude this extended journey into the heart of self-motivation, it is with the understanding that your symphony is unique, and your legacy is in the making. The additional chapters offer new dimensions to the ongoing exploration, providing you with tools to celebrate, adapt, collaborate, and craft a lasting impact.

Your journey of self-motivation is not confined to the pages of this book; it extends into the tapestry of your life. Each chapter, each reflection, each celebration contributes to the opus of your personal symphony.

As you continue your voyage, may you find inspiration in the wisdom of adaptability, the joy of celebration, the power of collaboration, and the enduring legacy you are crafting.

In this final reflection, consider the words of the late Maya Angelou: "**I've learned that people will forget what you said, people will forget what you did, but people will never forget how you made them feel**." Your journey of self-motivation is not just about what you achieve; it's about the impact you create and the feelings you evoke in yourself and others.

Thank you for allowing this exploration to be a part of your journey. As you carry the symphony of self-motivation forward, may your legacy resonate with the transformative power of internal guidance, sustained motivation, and the perpetual pursuit of a purpose-driven life.

The symphony continues, and the legacy unfolds. Your journey is both an individual odyssey and a shared narrative, contributing to the collective melody of self-motivation that echoes through time.

Conclusion: Embracing the Enchanting Magic of Transformation

Alright, fantastic reader, get ready for a deep dive into the magic pool of transformation! In these concluding pages, we're not just skimming the surface; we're plunging into the heart of your journey, where you're not just a reader—you're the main character in this spellbinding tale of self-discovery and change.

🚀 **Launching into Purposeful Living: **

Imagine your life as a rocket, ready to launch into purposeful living. It's time to break free from the everyday grind and embark on an exhilarating adventure. You're not just here to exist; you're here to live with intent and enthusiasm.

🧭 **Navigating Life's Twisty Path: **

Ever feel like life is a maze, and you're the one holding the map? Well, guess what? You have the power to navigate life's twisty paths. It's not about following the same old route; it's about carving your own, creating a story that's uniquely yours.

**Time – Your Invaluable Sidekick: **

Tick-tock! Time is your trusty sidekick in this adventure. It's more than just minutes and hours; it's a magical force. Grab it, savor it, and let it be the ally that propels you towards your dreams. You're the time-traveling hero of your own story.

**Forging a Heartfelt Connection with Your Existence: **

Life isn't just about going through the motions; it's about forging a heartfelt connection with your existence. Think of each day as a love letter to life itself. Fall in love with the journey and watch as your days transform into vibrant chapters of a love story.

**Cultivating Confidence Like a Growth Superpower: **

Picture this: you, standing tall and confident, like a superhero with an unbeatable power—confidence. It's not about being a different person; it's about cultivating the superhero within you. Growth is your superpower, and every challenge is an opportunity to level up.

**Real Stories, Real Sparks of Inspiration: **

Pause for a moment and dive into real stories— ordinary people achieving extraordinary things. These are not just stories; they are sparks of inspiration, igniting the flame of possibility within you. Real stories, real sparks, and you're part of this constellation of inspiration.

**Embarking on a Self-Motivation Expedition: **

The journey into self-motivation is like embarking on an expedition within your own heart and mind. It's about uncovering the treasures of your motivation, understanding what fuels your passion, and embracing the explorer within.

**Crafting Your Positive Energy Canvas: **

Imagine your mind as an artist's canvas, and you hold the brush dipped in positive energy. With each stroke, you're crafting a masterpiece of optimism. Your life becomes a gallery filled with vibrant hues of positivity, radiating an energy that transforms both you and the world around you.

**Answering the Call to Action: **

Enough with sitting on the sidelines, it's time to join the action-packed adventure called life. This book is your call to action, a superhero guide empowering you to jump into the ring and be the hero of your own story.

**Heartfelt Thanks for Surfing the Wisdom Waves: **

A tidal wave of gratitude crashes over you! Thank you for riding the waves of wisdom with me. Your time is not just appreciated; it's cherished. You've invested it in unlocking the secrets of a magical life, and for that, I'm sincerely thankful.

**Transformative Journey, Beyond the Pages: **

Hold on tight because this book isn't just a collection of words on pages. It's a transformative journey, and you're the protagonist. You're not merely reading; you're experiencing a metamorphosis, and the magic is extending beyond these very pages.

**Words that Echo in Your Heart: **

These words aren't just ink on paper; they're echoes in your heart. They're not merely letters; they're enchantments that resonate within you. Let them linger, let them guide you, and let them be the compass on your journey of self-discovery.

👉 **Infinite Adventures Await, Your Story Unfolds:

As we bid adieu to these pages, remember, this isn't the end—it's a beginning. Your life story is a book with infinite chapters waiting to unfold. You're not just the reader; you're the storyteller, and the best adventures are yet to come.

Ready to embrace the enchantment? Your journey has just begun.

<u>"Beyond Words: Overflowing with Gratitude - A Heartfelt Thank You to My Enchanting Readers"</u>

Dear wonderful & Amazing Readers,

A massive thanks to each one of you – my readers, students, family, mentors, seniors, colleagues, customers, and friends! Your gift of time, the most precious thing you have, spent reading this book, means the world to me.

"In these pages, I've shared the secrets of life's little wonders that wield significant impact. Now, I'm eagerly waiting to hear your thoughts, reviews, and feedback.

Let's connect! You can find me at **rahul11787@gmail.com**, and I'm excited to know how this small effort of mine resonates with you.

Connect with me on other platforms for more updates and insights:

🎥 YOUTUBE:

- [RAHULPARMAR_THE-STATE-BANKER]

(https://www.youtube.com/@RAHULPARMAR_THE-STATE-BANKER)

- [Josh Talks with Rahul]

(https://www.youtube.com/@JoshTalkswithRahul)

 YouTube handle: @RAHULPARMAR_THE-STATE-BANKER & @JoshTalkswithRahul

📘 FACEBOOK:

facebook.com/rahul11787

🐦 TWITTER:

twitter.com/rahul11787

📷 INSTAGRAM:

instagram.com/rahul11787

Let's stay connected on these platforms for more discussions, updates, and behind-the-scenes insights. Looking forward to engaging with you there!   "

In our journey together, we've explored the amazing impact of three special words – Love, Affection, and Gratitude. Imagine them as threads weaving through the story of life, guiding us toward something great. I've tried to show how these words can really change the way we live through stories and real-life stuff.

But wait, there's more magic waiting for you in these pages!

We've also unraveled the Power of Positive Attitude and Self-Belief – the secret sauce that can turn challenges into triumphs. It's like having a shield against negativity and a superpower to tackle life head-on.

Knowing the Value of Your Time is another key – the currency of life. We've delved into why it's crucial to spend it wisely, making each moment count. Time is like a magical ingredient that, when used wisely, can create a life filled with abundance.

Being an Action Taker and Avoiding Procrastination is the superhero move you need. We've explored the magic of taking that first step, the power of momentum, and how small actions can lead to big changes.

The Power of Imagination and Affirmation has been our guide to creating the life we want. It's like having a crystal ball to visualize success and using positive words to make it happen.

Dive into the Secret of the Law of Attraction – the invisible force that brings what we think about into our lives. We've explored how thoughts become things and how aligning our energy can attract the right vibes.

Powerful moments of Self-Realization have unfolded, urging you to understand yourself better. It's about embracing your strengths, acknowledging your areas of growth, and evolving into the best version of yourself. 🌱

And the grand finale – Be Your Own Mentor! This chapter is a celebration of your inner wisdom. It's about trusting your gut, making decisions with confidence, and realizing that you are your best guide. 👤

As we wrap up this magical journey, I extend my deepest thanks for being a part of it. Your time, thoughts, and reviews are treasures, and I can't wait to hear your insights.

Thanks for being part of this adventure! May the magic of Love, Affection, Gratitude, Positive Attitude, Self-Belief, Time Value, Action-Taking, Imagination, Affirmation, Law of Attraction, Self-Realization, and Being Your Own Mentor continue to light up your path. Here's to a fantastic New Year filled with positive changes! 🎉

Your success is my joy. If, by any chance, this book contributes to your wins, drop me a line via email or reviews. Your stories are real gems, and I genuinely salute you from the bottom of my heart.

Wishing you a fantastic and Very Happy New Year! May it mark a turning point in your life, filled with success and positivity.

Stay safe, happy, and successful wherever you are. Be a shining example, excel, and let the world know the brilliance of India.

Jai Hind! Jai Bharat!

With a heart full of gratitude,

Rahul Parmar

Author, State Banker & Motivational Speaker

Bangalore (Karnataka), India